Who Am I?

What Am I?

What Do I Want To Be

...When I Grow Up?

*A YOUNG MAN'S SCRATCH AND
SNIFF GUIDE THRU PUBERTY*

TOM NORTHAM

Copyright © 2019 Thomas E Northam. All rights reserved.

To my son, Jerome

Table of Contents

Chapter One   Respect and How to Get It

Chapter Two   Clean Up Your Act!

Chapter Three   Clothing

Chapter Four   Etiquette

Chapter Five   Table Settings and Manners

Chapter Six   Shoe Box Management

Chapter Seven   Substance Abuse

Chapter Eight   Money Management

Chapter Nine   Learning to Communicate

Chapter Ten   Spirituality

Chapter Eleven   Sexuality

Chapter Twelve   Who Am I? What Am I? What Do I Want to Be   When I Grow Up?

Chapter Thirteen   Preparing to Live on Your Own

Preface

Do you feel like you don't fit in or people don't accept you? Are there times when you don't know just what to do or you feel a little awkward? We've all had them at some time or another, and we will in the future as well. This book is not intended to cover all those times but will greatly help with many. Boys, from ages ten, eleven or twelve until about age eighteen are going through a change...it is called puberty. I jokingly refer to it as the "charming age of puberty," but it is not a joke. It is a very difficult time and one that is not too often talked about — especially if you are a boy. There isn't much written to help boys. You are going through a transition from a boy to a young man. There are a lot of changes, some more subtle than others. It's happening in your body and your mind. It often is referred to as "maturing."

The physical change is the most noticeable. Your voice changes, you start to grow hair from new places, body parts begin to grow and develop; there is a host of things. You begin to "fill-out." Emotionally, you become very sensitive, find yourself attracted to others, question yourself and others.

Conscience is that wee-small voice in the back of your head that tells you whether something is right or wrong. You need to learn to listen to it and make the right choices. Life is a series of choices. It's okay to be who you are, and you can be what you want to be. These are your choices and you alone must make them.

In some regards, it's like a game of cards—we must play with the hand that is dealt us. Some play by the rules, others don't. Some win, the rest don't — they lose. During my lifetime, I've been a winner and a loser. Being a winner is far better, and being able to choose your own destiny is better yet.

Some play the "If and Only" hand, and others play the "What If?" hand. Still others just play the Joker. The "If and Only" hand blames the situation on others: "If only this hadn't happened...if only that hadn't happened. It's not my fault; it's only because of this or that. What if I'd won the lottery?" Don't blame the other guy for your own choices. You made them all. Others just joke around and get nowhere.

This book is designed for those who want to make the right choices. It is a compilation of facts that can help you to be acceptable in the social and work world, to come across in a professional manner and make decisions that guide your destiny. It will not provide the answer for all things but will help you to be accepted and earn people's respect. After all, isn't that what it's all about?

There is an old saying: "You can lead a horse to water, but you can't make it drink." You can use these suggestions and guidance or not. It's up to you' it's your choice.

We are all looking for acceptance and respect. We're also trying to figure out how to do that. Who are we and what does it take to gain either one? How do we get through this awkward period of our lives, somewhere between being a child and a young man?

Who Am I? What Am I? What Do I Want To Be When I Grow Up? is an outgrowth of a pamphlet I wrote to provide guidance for the male students in the Youth Opportunity Program (YOP). This program was established by the federal government to help the children of lower-income families in the workplace. These young people were called "YOPs." Most of them were between ages sixteen to eighteen and would work a couple of hours two or three days a week after school and full-time during the summer months.

The YOPs at Port Hueneme, a naval base in southern California, were mostly children of migrant farm workers or divorced parents who were trying to make a living. In many cases, the parents or guardians didn't have or take the time to provide good or wise counsel. In many cases, they didn't know themselves what to do. Whatever the case, the kids simply didn't know.

When the YOPs started their job, they were given tasks geared toward obtaining knowledge and developing skills and abilities. For this, they would clear, after taxes, about $40 every other week. In many cases, it was the first $40 they had ever seen. This was in 1967, and the girls would head out and blow their whole check on a wig or something impractical. The boys did similarly by purchasing an expensive shirt, never realizing the need to clean it, and it would soon become apparent to all around that they hadn't.

At Port Hueneme, John Robert Powers professional models would come in to teach the girls about cleanliness and how to wisely spend money on necessities, and about "girly things." I became aware that there was no such program for the boys.

As a Division Director for the Naval Ship Missile Systems Engineering Station (NSWSES) and an actor and entertainer in the area, I was fairly well known. Having struggled during my own youth, I felt compelled to put together a list of "dos" and "don'ts" to guide the boys through this difficult time in their lives — guidance and information on that which is not generally taught in public schools. I developed a pamphlet entitled "For Young Men Only," which I provided to each of the male YOPs, along with a 45-minute lecture. It was well received and was soon adopted by the federal government in the Port Hueneme area, the Ventura County School System along with the Camarillo State Mental Hospital.

Although I wrote the original pamphlet over fifty years earlier, most of its guidance still applies today. Of course, the budget estimates were drastically changed and there are many new technologies; however, common sense and good manners have never varied. It has now been updated and expanded to include new technologies and those issues which need to be addressed. It has proven to be a very useful and effective reference in the past, and I'm sure will in the future.

It is my sincere wish that it will help someone along life's journey.

Chapter One — Respect and How to Get It

You are the product of your past experiences and environment. You are you — you are who you are, and that's okay. However, if you want to better yourself and get along in the world, there may be a few things you might want to change.

When I was in my teens and several years beyond those days, I didn't have a clue as to who I was. I really hadn't thought about it. I did know that at fourteen I was still treated as a child, which I resented. When I was sixteen to eighteen, I was still treated like some irresponsible twit. Why was this? Perhaps I was acting like an irresponsible twit! My parents and others just didn't understand me. Does this sound familiar?

What is it that you want — respect? We all do, and to gain the respect of others, we must be respectful of others. Maybe we need to look at what respect is? First, for others to respect you, you need to respect yourself. Take pride in all you do.

Today the Internet, with Facebook, Instagram, Messenger, Twitter, etc., has expanded our abilities to communicate, to learn, and to stay informed on most anything. It provides so much that is positive in life. It's a Good News/Bad News situation for while it provides many opportunities, it also increases the chance for exposure, self-destruction and the loss of self-respect. For once something is posted, it never goes away. What may be amusing or fun today, may not be so humorous later. What pictures you post today, you may not think was so wise in a few minutes, for like your record, these actions will follow you the rest of your life. Too many times what you think you sent to one person, ends up being shared with the world. Once something is on the Internet, it will always be there. It is out there -- FOREVER!

So, you need to respect yourself first. You do this through accomplishment, achievement and advancement. The best organization to help you do this is the Boy Scouts of America. For the young boy until age 17, in some cases 20, there is no finer organization in the world. They are well organized and have extensive programs in virtually any field you can imagine and help you get there. They help you find interests and hobbies and introduce you to a wide range of activities. They have developed 135 Merit Badges, which range from American Business and Arts to Wilderness Survival and Woodworking. Look online for the Boy Scout Council nearest you, contact your unit, complete your application, and begin.

One of the best sources of showing respect is the Boy Scouts of America's Scout Law which spells it out: we should be *trustworthy, loyal, helpful, friendly, courteous, kind, obedient, cheerful, thrifty, brave, clean, and reverent.*

It's hard to live all these things today, just like it was yesterday or will be tomorrow. But you must try. These are commands, goals and objectives. So are laws; they tell us what is acceptable and what isn't, and there is a penalty if we make the wrong choice or decision. That can result in three different ways: 1) We don't get caught and consider ourselves lucky; 2) we do get caught, and there are consequences — either by paying a heavy fine or we go to jail, which can destroy your life; or 3) sometimes we get off with community service which can be an embarrassment or could complicate our lives. It's easier to do the right thing.

Respect is the first thing we are searching for and in order to gain respect, we must be respectful—we must respect others, and we might as well get this out of the way right now. To the responsible person, there is nothing more disrespectful than staring into a cell phone or mobile device...
They have no place in the art of face-to-face communication with anyone.

Cell Phones and Other Mobile Devices

The use of cell or mobile phones is increasingly the source of convenience—also disruption and irritation. Many people are tethered to them; they have become slaves to their devices. They also are oblivious to what's going on around them, and seemingly don't care. Most have become totally disrespectful of others.

Not too long ago a friend called and asked if I would take his daughter and a girlfriend out on our boat. I told him I would gladly do so. I spent about an hour getting the boat ready and loaded it with lunch, snacks and soft drinks.

When they arrived, we got on the boat and pushed away from our dock and headed out of the cove onto the main lake. The two girls were both seventeen and using their cell phones. They were texting. As it turned out, they were texting each other. I pointed out something about the lake and they both ignored what I was saying. They were totally absorbed into their own world and their texting to each other. I turned the boat around and headed back to our boat dock.

After docking, they looked up. They looked a little confused and surprised when I said that the tour was over. I then said, *"Don't ever expect me to take you out again...or should I text that to you?"*

They got the message and the ones father was totally embarrassed and they left. What could have been a nice couple of hours on the boat and lunch, turned into embarrassment and nothing. All due to disrespect, rudeness and cell phones.

Rule of Thumb: Do the right thing. Be polite.

Chapter Two — Clean Up Your Act!

Personal Hygiene and Appearance

The first and foremost step of being accepted is what you look like and how pleasant it is to be around you. Your appearance is one of the prime factors of acceptance. People judge and formulate an opinion of you by your appearance. If your appearance doesn't meet their standards, chances are you will be rejected. They will never know whether you are okay or not. It probably isn't the way things should be, but it is the way things are. Therefore, whether you worry about how you look or not — you should. We are going to address this in more detail later and make recommendations.

Let's take one of the Boy Scout Code words and check it out: *clean*.

Personal Cleanliness: We've all had health education or personal hygiene in school at some point: wash your hands, brush your teeth, etc. Today, with everything going on, it is easy to forget that we have this responsibility to ourselves and to others.

First, each of us has our own odor. Whether it's our hair, mouth, arm pits, hands, crotch, butt or feet. Each emits odors. The degree of control we exercise through cleanliness over these odors determines how pleasant we are to be around. There is absolutely no excuse for being offensive. My maternal grandmother told me, *"It is no sin to be poor; it is to be dirty."*

Fortunately, science has offered several solutions to this problem: Bacterial and deodorant soaps, shampoos, deodorant, toothpaste, colognes, hand lotions and foot powders. These are sold for the purpose of controlling, correcting and improving human odors. There are no exceptions, we all stink at some time or another. Usually we are the last to notice. There are people whose breath is so bad that I avoid going near to them. It's not right that I do that, but I do.

For example, a lot of people love garlic and onions. All retain some of it. Others exude it from every pore. My son can eat garlic, and I can tell it within an hour, and this is for the rest of the day. As a result, he avoids garlic. Second hand garlic smell is totally offensive to most people.

To a lesser degree, onions can have the same impact. I love onions and become very self-conscious about what my breath smells like. The same is true with coffee with cream and sugar. It leaves a film on your tongue. Brushing your tongue won't help; you must scrape it. The only way to remove this is by scraping. That is why they make tongue-scrapers. Most dentists will give you one if you ask. They also have them in Walmart and many other stores.

Let's run through the rest of the list of possible offenders.

Showers and Bathing: In some areas of our country, people are rural and still using a water pump, a bucket, a wood stove, and they wash in a basin, which in turn is carried out and the water pitched.

Others have running water, and hot water at that. I think it is safe to say we all have showers, although there are those who do not use them as often as they should. Get in and soap up with a good bar of unscented deodorant soap from head to toe. This includes every part of your body: your ears, neck, under your arms, your privates including your butt-crack and feet including between your toes.

This removes all the body oils that accumulate over the day or so since the last bath. These same oils attract dirt and dust as well as perspiration. This causes body odor.

Hair Care: Bathing also includes your hair, whether its soap or preferably shampoo, for it too accumulates oils and smells. Soap will make your scalp dry and flaky, so you're better off with shampoo. For those with dandruff, I have only found one shampoo that will control it, and that is Head and Shoulders. If you use hair spray or Brylcreem, often referred to as "greasy kid stuff" hair dressing, it is even more important. For those who use pomades like Murray's Hair Dressing Pomade or Royal Crown Hair Dressing Pomade, more frequent washing is recommended to avoid bad odor.

With today's tendencies to have longer hair, we sometimes avoid shampooing our hair because it combs better with a little oil on it. Believe me, it doesn't smell better.

Toileting: There is no good time to discuss the following; however, it needs to be said. There are some things that are constant and normal — going to the toilet. Urinating or peeing, is one, and often referred to as "No. 1." Being a male, urinating can be done standing up. That's what a urinal is for in public restrooms. Stand close to it and aim down; otherwise, it can splatter urine back onto your pants or coats, often leaving you with wet spots. By standing close, you avoid dripping on the floor. The same goes in your home, where you only have a toilet fixture. Stand completely over the toilet to avoid dripping on the floor. Also, be careful not to splatter onto the surrounding walls, which need to be cleaned and generally are not which can create a bad odor in the bathroom. It is okay to sit to urinate, and many men do, thus avoiding splattering.

Bowel movements ("BM's"), often referred to as "No. 2," are something that needs to be addressed as well. Whether in public restrooms or private bathrooms, there are things that you need to be aware of. 1) After passing the feces or waste from your body, flush the toilet. This is called a "courtesy flush" and quickly eliminates the odor. You may need to do this more than once. 2) Clean-up or wiping is done by using toilet tissue or paper. In many countries, they do not have rolled toilet paper or tissue, but cut up and used newspapers or magazines. 3) **Do not** roll off wads of toilet paper; roll off four or five small sheets in a single strip and fold it neatly to clean yourself. Repeat until you no longer need to. Some people wad up an abundance of paper which not only needlessly wastes the paper, but can plug up the toilet fixture, causing it to overflow. 4) Some people have a package of "flushable wipes" available on the water tank of the toilet fixture. These are for final cleaning and are limited to one per flush. They are a moist and scented dissolvable fiber or paper-like wipe that thoroughly cleans.

Regardless, always flush the toilet. If there are feces marks in the bowl after flushing, there is often a small long-handled brush in a container usually just back of the toilet fixture. Use the brush to eliminate the marks and re-flush after returning the brush to the container.

Caution: When using public restrooms, always clean the seat with toilet tissue and use a protective seat tissues provided for that purpose (referred to as "seat covers"). Several diseases are transmitted via the toilet seat, primarily herpes.

Always wash your hands after toileting. In many cases, it is wise to wash your hands before and after, in that you handle yourself while toileting and can transfer germs or dirt.

Deodorants: There are a lot of deodorants on the market, some better than others. I prefer the unscented ones. I also prefer the spray style as the stick deodorants get all over the inside of your shirt and turns the armpits yellow. It doesn't come out very easily. Experiment and find the deodorant that controls perspiration.

Oral Hygiene: Nothing beats brushing one's teeth. Brushing your tongue does nothing but smear it around. It takes a tongue scraper. One doesn't hear about them too often; however, they still make them, and you'll be amazed at what comes out of your mouth. It is the leading cause of bad breath.

You should brush three times a day, but that isn't always possible. This doesn't mean you have to carry a toothbrush around with you, just be aware. A good mouthwash is also generally required. Get into the habit of brushing, scraping your tongue, and then rinsing with mouthwash. You will be happy you did and so will the people you speak to. Breath mints are a good thing to carry with you. If you are offered one, take it.

Fingernails: Wash your hands regularly! When you think about where they have been and what they have done, there should be no hesitation. However, we forget to wash them. Especially if you've been working in grease or paint. Scrub them with a good soap and hand brush. If this doesn't do it, use an old toothbrush and cleanser. Get your fingernails clean, for there is no excuse for dirty fingernails. Nothing looks worse or more unkempt. Even worse is the person who bites their nails and doesn't clean them. If you bite your nails, make a concerted effort to quit. It gives the appearance of having psychological difficulties or not well adjusted. It can also lead to deformity of your fingers. There are products in the pharmacy that will help with this problem. Ask the pharmacists.

Foot Care: Some people have problems with their feet, others don't. Athletes foot is not exclusive or selective; it is common and uncomfortable and is easily spread, especially in a gymnasium or showers. In a bad case, a doctor should be seen. For minor conditions, and for small raw, itchy areas, there are many fine powders on the market. Ask a pharmacist. Old socks stink! Change them.

You see, there is a lot involved with the simple word "*clean*." You must do them all, for it shows you respect yourself and others as well.

Just as your body needs cleaning, so do your clothes. What good is it if you have a clean body and put dirty clothes back on? You may be clean, but your clothes are dirty. It's hard to tell which is which? You still smell, you stink.

Change your socks and underwear every day if that's possible. Make sure your shirt is clean as well as your pants. Clean your shoes. All these draw attention to you. If they're clean and you're clean, people notice. If there is an odor, everyone notices.

Let's look at *"helpful."* Included in this is doing the laundry. You can't expect someone to do your's and pick up after you. It doesn't take a great talent to keep your room straight and clean. Just pick it up, and throw it in a laundry basket if you have one, or better yet, take it to the washing machine and learn how to run it. Take responsibility for yourself. You'll be respected for it.

Don't expect others to do things for you that you can do yourself. I remember a young boy riding a bicycle and pitching an empty container of coke on the street. I said, *"Who do you think is going to pick that up?"* He replied in a smart-mouth manner, *"the janitor,"* to which I responded that we didn't have one. He drove past and then came back to pick it up. He thought about what I said, and then felt guilty. He did the right thing.

Grooming: Included in "clean" is grooming. The rule of thumb here is to do the best you can with what you've got. Dress sharp, stand up straight, and take care of your body, you're going to be looking at it for a long time.

Haircuts: Today, there is no leading trend to hair length. Some wear it long and others shave their head. There is nothing wrong with any of them. Extra-long hair looks cheap and dirty and generally is. Haircuts are not cheap so plan on getting it cut now and then. Unkempt hair is a sign that you don't care what you look like. Keep the hair on your lower neck trimmed.

Facial Care: Take care of your face. Wash daily with a good soap and thoroughly rinse. As a young man you are either going through or about to encounter "puberty." It is the time when hormones are changing, and hair is beginning to grow from new places.

This is also the time when your skin can develop acne, white or black heads and other conditions. Don't let it get out of hand. Keep it clean and check with a doctor about possible treatments. It is also a time if you don't take care of it, permanent scarring can occur.

Skin Care: Common skin conditions are oily skin which can result in black heads, white heads or acne, and dry skin, each of which may have different reactions. Dry skin conditions are sometimes referred to as "ashen" skin and is common among African Americans. This can be controlled by the application of Vaseline or petroleum jelly. All unusual conditions should be checked by a dermatologist so it doesn't get worse.

Shaving: Beards, moustaches, and sideburns look good in movies and on stage, not in school nor in the workplace. Shaving and bathing go together. Sideburns should be classically even with the bead of your ear.

Eyebrows: Some develop hair between their eyebrows, and are called a unibrow, meaning the appearance of having one very long eyebrow. Some will shave above their noses to eliminate the unibrow look. Most will pluck the unwanted hair out with tweezers which pulls the hair out by the roots. Plucking is better, in that it will eventually stop hair growing where it isn't wanted. One can buy a pair of tweezers which simulates scissors and are easy to work with.

Chest Hair: Many will start to grow chest hair. Don't shave it off, for it will come in even more thickly and will grow longer. Just leave it alone...it's manly.

Fingernails: Should be clean, trimmed and filed, and never longer than the tip of your fingers. Trim them and don't bite your nails.

Cologne: While there are a lot of nice smelling colognes or after shaves on the market, they should be used sparingly — if at all, and never to avoid taking a bath. Caution: Many people are very allergic to them, particularly asthmatics. When you use colognes, use after a shower or bath and put just a drop behind each ear in the soft area just below your ear. Usually, the more pleasant colognes are very expensive, e.g., $75 and up. However, there are a few that are affordable and pleasant smelling such as: Brut, English Leather, Old Spice, Bay Rum, Aqua Velva, to mention a few.

Tattoos: Getting a tattoo is currently a fad or phase and appears to be in style. Think about it long and hard, for once applied, there is no going back. Talk to someone who already has one and ask if they would do it again. Many are proud of their tattoos and many others wouldn't do it again. If you already have a tattoo, be aware that there are many people who are completely turned-off by them. If you are looking for a job, do yourself a favor and make an effort to hide your tattoo if you are being interviewed. Wear a long-sleeved shirt or jacket to hide it, or you will probably not be hired for a professional position.

Although you hear talk of laser removal; it is twice the cost of the tattoo and doesn't work very well. There is always a trace of the tattoo or there is scarring. Maybe it's my years in entertainment, but I cannot imagine getting a tattoo, for you are limiting what you can do and what people will think about you for the rest of your life.

Body Piercing: This is a no brainer! Why poke holes in your body? I call it self-mutilation and once done, there is no turning back, your body is permanently scarred. Real men don't wear earrings or pierce their bodies — anyplace. Those who do, are seeking attention. Just like tattoos, you are destroying your body. Garner attention by being respectful of others. Your body is a temple; treat is as such. Respect your body for it has to last a long time. I've seen men with their ears ripped off and others with champagne corks embedded in their ear lobes. I've seen others with rings through their nipples. Once in NYC, I saw one character with a bolt and washers through both his cheeks and saw people turn away gagging. I've seen pierced eyebrows and eyelids — and for what purpose? It isn't cool, brave or attractive; it is repulsive. It is also running the risk of damaging yourself and creating exposure to infection, and it shows ignorance and stupidity.

Clothing Care: Clothing should be clean, pressed and worn as designed. Shirts designed to be tucked in should be and those that weren't shouldn't be. Pants should be worn around your waist, not around your thighs or below your butt. Shoes should be polished and/or clean.

Neatness in appearance is as essential as cleanliness—it reflects character and will determine what people think of you. They just might begin to show you some respect. Because as you begin to "clean up your act" you will be respectable. Who can't respect that?

You are starting to become someone other than the person you thought you were. You are growing up!

A Dopp Kit for Toilet Articles

A **Dopp Kit or Travel Kit or Toilet Kit or Shaving Kit (all the same thing).** *It is a must for the rest of your life.* Get used to it. If you don't shave yet, be glad. Also, don't let peach fuzz linger. Shave it off. A Dopp Kit is to hold all your toiletries for grooming. These come in all sizes and varieties and from plastic to fine leather. Costs can vary from around ten dollars to hundreds of dollars. The one pictured above is the most common type.

Organize it and keep your toiletries together so you don't have to quickly put everything back in it. If you keep it all together, all you have to do is grab the handle and go.

Toilet Articles

The following articles are essential for good grooming and will help you to always be prepared:

- Electric razor, cordless, or
- Razor with blades, disposable. Keep it in a plastic bag.
- Shave Cream, tube
- Styptic pencil, if you nick yourself shaving
- Deodorant, unscented
- Toothpaste
- Mouthwash, small
- Toothbrush and case
- Tongue Scraper
- Dental Floss
- Toothpicks, small packet*
- Chapstick or similar product for chapped lips

- Comb

- Shampoo or appropriate hair cleaner or Head and Shoulders, small bottle

- Soap, deodorant, unscented with plastic case

- Skin cream or lotion for dry skin

- Fingernail brush

- Fingernail clip

- Fingernail file

- Small ziploc bag of band-aids for emergencies, one or two

- [Foot Powder, if you have a problem]

* I carry a small Swiss Army Knife in my pocket which has a toothpick, a pair of tweezers, scissors, and a nail file, as well as a knife.

Start by purchasing a Dopp Kit, and then as you buy things, add them to your Kit. An electric razor starts at around $40 and can go to $100+. They are a lot easier, but also expensive.

👍 **Rule of Thumb: Take care of your body, it's the only one you will ever have.**

For additional information and instructions for shaving and other grooming, check out the website theartofmanliness.com.

Chapter Three — Clothing

A major component of your appearance is clothing. Not everyone has a large wardrobe. Clothes cost money, which is something few have to throw around. When purchasing clothes, there are two schools of thought: 1) do I want to be in style? or 2) do I want something that will last and look nice? They can be mutually exclusive. I prefer the latter. Fad clothes are just that; they are the current fad and won't last.

Quality clothes are always acceptable and usually in style. They can be worn year in and year out. Most fad clothes are here today and gone tomorrow. All cost money. I would rather spend money to have something that will last. Take care of them and they *will* take care of you.

Another thing to consider in purchasing clothes, are they dry clean only or are they washable? Dry cleaning is expensive, and it doesn't take more than two or three dry cleaning to pay for a new one. Some shirts are prime targets for having to dry clean.

Because they are expensive to dry clean, we don't too often and soon you can smell the wearer coming. Read the labels. Avoid 100% polyester, as it is hot to wear and, because of this, it absorbs odor. Leather falls into the same category.

If you find a brand of shirt that is cotton blend, say 80% cotton and 20% polyester, that is permanent press which you like, stick with it. At the end of this chapter is a list of items which I put together for young men who had their first jobs working for the federal government. Regardless of where you work, there are some things you can do and others you shouldn't do, some clothes you should wear and others you *definitely* should not.

When you don't have a lot of money, you must plan what to wear. Buy things that fall into the same color spectrum. Buy things that you can mix and match. What I'm recommending is for building a wardrobe, starting with the basics, and then building from there.

Underwear: Use full T-shirts as opposed to the tank-top or sleeveless undershirt. A full T-shirt will act as an absorbent for perspiration and will prevent soiling and damage to dress or sport shirts. They can also be worn with a pair of shorts. As for underpants, use what you are comfortable wearing, but change daily.

Socks: Pick a color that blends with shirts and slacks. Dark, plain socks are desirable. Avoid designs and bright colors. If foot problems exist, use only white cotton sport socks until it clears up. Buy black and brown or tan dress socks. They should match your slacks or your shoes. I use cover the calf. The tan socks go well with cotton tan or khaki semi-dress pants.

Shirts: With today's permanent press or no-iron fabrics, half of your problems are solved. They don't wrinkle. With a clean body and underclothing, a shirt can be worn several times before laundering. Therefore, select plain shirts. Use basic styles of shirts, avoid gimmicks, monograms, patterns and other memorable or distinctive styles. The reason is that people remember them and know if you wore it yesterday or for several days in a row.

A plain white, button-down collared shirt has many uses. It can be sport and dress combined. It always looks fresh and clean—barring accidents. If you can only afford one shirt, make it a white, short-sleeved, button-down collar, permanent no-iron shirt. Colored sport shirts should be selected to color coordinate with slacks and in a basic style. Avoid distinctive styles and patterns. A good choice for a second shirt would be a long-sleeve, light blue button-down color. This can also be worn as a dress shirt.

Slacks or Pants: Everyone should have one pair of blue jeans and one pair of light tan or khaki cotton semi-dress slacks, like Docker's, which are permanent-press. Both are washable. Once you have them stick to navy, black or brown dress slack. Go to most any department store and try them on. Kohl's, Belk, Macy's, Walmart, they all have them. If you are thin, get the flat front. Stick with solid colors without pattern. Another alternative is a pair of cords which can be worn for nearly all occasions.

Suits, Sport Coats, Jackets and Sweaters: If I had but one choice, it would be a navy-blue blazer with brass buttons. It would be nice to have all the above, but sometimes that isn't possible. The blazer can be worn with blue jeans, tan and khaki slacks, informal or formal. If you have a pair of navy slacks, it can be worn and becomes a suit. It is by far the most versatile. When buying a sports jacket or suit, stick with plain colors and avoid odd textures or loud colors. Keep it simple. When you buy a sweater, buy a standard style. Watch for sales and stick with good stores, but don't forget to check Goodwill Industries or other second-hand clothing stores. Good items for a fraction of the cost.

Shoes: These are probably the only articles of clothing that require constant care and have an initially high cost. Therefore, purchase a plain round-toed, basic black or brown or oxblood colored oxford or slip-on loafer. Keep them well polished. Take care of them and they will take care of you for a long time. A well-polished shoe goes with anything and will off-set any outfit you're wearing. Avoid fad-type shoes, because they're here today and gone tomorrow. A good shoe will run about $65+. For sportswear, or just running around, use tennis or sport shoes or similar that you can wash. They require virtually no care yet look good.

Accessories: Buy belts to match your pant colors. They do make a one-inch belt that is brown on one side and black on the other -- convertible ($25). Avoid belts with large or flashy buckles.

Get two medium width ties that coordinate with your sports coat and slacks. 100% silk ties cost around $60, so this is something to look for at Goodwill Industries or a second-hand shop.

Cuff links are primarily for evening wear but buy simple ones. Avoid the flashy, oversized or jeweled ones.

A sports cap or a baseball cap should be worn as designed with the visor or bill of the cap in front. Otherwise it looks geeky. Never sit at a table and wear a hat.

Note*: Carry a small pocket knife, such as a Swiss Army (about $20) with small blades and toothpick and tweezers for emergencies. A small coin purse will prevent coins from wearing a hole in your pocket. If you are fortunate enough to travel, going through the* *airports can be a hassle. Put your coins and other items in snack-size Ziploc bags so they can be easily extracted and put in the trays. Do not take your pocket knife on the plane in your pocket or carry-on — use your check-in luggage for this.*

Clothing – "Should Haves"

The following list of clothing articles should be viewed as a guideline or foundation for building a complete wardrobe. It should not be considered the maximum, rather the minimum.

2   White dress shirts, button down collars, no-iron

2   Colored sport shirts, button down collars, no-iron

1   Dress slacks – Dockers khakis or light tan permanent press

1   Jeans, *not with holes nor patches nor fade marks*

1   Sports shorts

1   Sports cap or baseball cap

1   Sport coat, navy blue blazer

2   Neck ties

1   Pair dress shoes

1   Pair casual or sports shoes (make sure they are washable)

6   Sets underwear

1   Set of pjamas

1   Pair of slippers

6   Pair socks

1   Sweater, dress with v-neck or crew neck

1   Windbreaker

1   Winter coat

1   Raincoat or folding umbrella

6   Handkerchiefs, to have for emergencies

1   Reversible belt, black or brown

1   Swim suit or sports shorts

1   Dopp Kit for toiletries

There are a lot of sources for clothing. Do not forget consignment shops, Goodwill Industries, or Salvation Army. These are great for finding bargains at considerably less costs.

> ***Rule of Thumb:** Shop wisely, you can save a lot of money.*

Chapter Four — Etiquette

Etiquette is a word used to establish "standards" or socially acceptable mannerisms, in other words, manners. Good manners are always a good policy and necessary. There is no place or time when this is not true. Especially as you began to grow up, you need to develop mannerisms and good habits as you enter the adult world. Whether you are entering the workplace and searching for a part-time or full-time job, developing friendships or beginning to date or just attending a social event the same rules apply. The basis of these rules is always consideration for the feelings, beliefs and sensibilities of others.

Good manners or bad ones are revealed in everything we are, have or do. Our speech, mannerisms, dress, the things that we are surrounded by—even our friendships are evidence of our inner-being and true self.

So far, your exposure to life has been limited to family and friends, church and activities, social clubs or scouting, and to school and related events. The emphasis on etiquette in most cases has been somewhat lax. Although we've all been subject to some restrictions on our manners and how we act. There are rules about home, friends, church, school, and so forth. We know what we can do and can't do — or one would hope!

Over the years, some of the rules change, but for the most part, good manners and bad have remained constant. For example, always hold the door for a female — even if it's your sister! That is called respect, and to gain respect, we must be respectful and respectable. It may seem like such a small thing, but it reflects who we are.

We are going to address many environments; however, there are some overall rules that apply. Each has its origins, but we'll just call them "Rules of Thumb." The first two are just common sense, but need to be addressed:

Do personal things in private. There are many personal necessities which people must perform such as burping or farting (formally known as passing gas); blowing your nose; scratching or picking anything, combing your hair, cleaning or trimming your fingernails or toenails, etc. Keep them private. They are neither interesting nor entertaining to anyone —anytime. They are just plain rude and offensive.

Smoking. If you don't smoke, don't start. There is nothing cool or glamorous about it. It is expensive and will destroy your health. If you must smoke, do it outside. Be aware that everyone can smell it on your clothes, hair, body and breath, and it stains your teeth. It stinks, even if you can't smell it.

As a general rule to just fit in or get by, avoid the subjects of sex, religion, politics, money, or anything that may be offensive to others. Be prepared to discuss any or all of the above in case you are asked your opinion. Sometimes they cannot be avoided, but be careful.

Never use foul or offensive language.

Always speak clearly and distinctly.

Always greet people with a smile and greeting: "Hello," "Hi," "How are you?," "Beautiful day," etc. all work fine. Always give your first and last name when introducing yourself or being introduced. "Hi, I'm John Smith, how are you?" Nothing is worse than to just say "Hello," when being introduced to someone. If someone is introducing you to someone who is older, respond with a Mr. or Mrs. and his or her last name. If they are introduced or are introducing themselves by their first name, it is all right to respond in kind, regardless of age. If you are being introduced and they only use your first name, it is perfectly okay to interject your full name even if they have already given part of it. Quite possibly, they have forgotten your whole name. For example: "Bill, this is John." It is okay to interject, "John Smith, glad to meet you."

Talk directly to the person you are addressing and look him or her in the eye. Nothing is more disconcerting to the recipient of a conversation than someone talking to the floor or looking around. Looking down tends to reveal that you either don't know and are lying. Looking around means you're not interested and looking for someone else to talk to or you don't want to be where you are.

Always leave with a departing comment. Say "Goodbye" or express your pleasure in meeting them. When leaving a conversation or departing, tell a person that it's been nice meeting or talking with him or her. The exception to this is at a reception or large gathering. It's okay to just leave.

OFFICE OR WORK RULES: Whether in a teacher's office, the principal, in the church or wherever, in an office environment the above rules still apply, but there are additional rules which need to be addressed. Often you will be given certain rules which must be observed. These may vary according to the environment or between jobs. The following are general rules which should be observed — just in case.

Never shout, speak loudly, or laugh excessively. You're not there to have fun.

Except for greeting, only speak when spoken to. Otherwise keep quiet. The best rule: listen and learn. Always be polite.

Address people by their title. It should always be Mr., Mrs., Miss, or Sir and Ma'am. Observe this until told to do otherwise. This applies on the telephone as well.

Only enter an office when asked. Never barge into someone's office. Wait at the door or entrance until you are invited to enter.

Never interrupt or intrude on a conversation. Be aware of what's going on around you. If two people are in conversation, never interrupt or intrude on their privacy. If something is of great importance, excuse yourself, state your business and wait for a response, or leave.

Stand until told to be seated. Never walk into someone's office and sit. Wait until they indicate what you should do. Stand or sit upright and be alert.

> ***Rule of Thumb: Remember the Golden Rule: He who has the gold makes the rules.***

Chapter Five — Table Settings and Manners

Table manners are very important and reflect a lot about you. Even more important is the respect you show those around you. There is no excuse or reason to exercise bad eating manners. Just because all around you may not observe the rules, can never be the reason for eating like a slob, it is neither cute nor funny. So, learn to eat the right way, practice it and you will always get along, regardless of where you go.

You have seen signs that say: *"No shirt, no shoes. No Service."* In short, if you are not properly dressed, don't come in. How you act in a restaurant or with others, is showing respect to all around you. This includes people at different tables; people you may not know. They may be out for a special occasion, or to discuss something work related and very concerning to them. It may be a couple celebrating their engagement. It's special. Would you want someone sitting next to you that is loud, or dirty, smelly—or wearing a hat? It makes no difference whether it's McDonald's, Burger King or the Ritz-Carlton dining room.

One of the most embarrassing things is to go for a nice dinner with a boss or a date and be seated at a table that is already properly set, and not knowing what to do with what's there. Below are two place settings. The first is for a more formal setting which one wouldn't normally find at McDonald's or the local dinner. Study it and learn what is placed where.

Napkin Bread & Butter Dish Wine Glass Water Goblet
Butter Knife

Photo by Thomas E. Northam
Cocktail Fork Dinner Fork Soup Bowl Knife Teaspoon Soup Spoon
Salad Fork Dinner Plate Charger

Formal Dinner Setting

This is the proper way to set a table in the United States of America. This is a formal setting typical of nicer restaurants or in a home when soup is the first course. If a salad is also served, it would go to the left of the forks. When eating, you always take silverware or flatware from the outside and work your way towards the center.

Bread & Butter Plate   Butter Knife   Water Glass

Salad Plate

Salad Fork
Dinner Fork

Dinner Plate
Charger
Dinner Knife
Teaspoon
Napkin

Photo by Thomas E. Northam

Informal Dinner Setting

This is the proper way to set a table in the home, although it is also used in restaurants as well. It is when a salad is served and is an informal setting. Once again, you always take silverware or flatware from the outside and work your way towards the center. This referred to as a family setting. If you were visiting someone and they asked you to set the table, this is the format that you would use.

Here are three rules up front, whether in a restaurant or in someone's home:

Always remove your hat when indoors, and always at the table.

Always shut your cell phone OFF, and keep it OFF. No one wants to hear your phone or text notices, or conversations.

If you have dietary restrictions, notify the host or hostess when you are invited to dinner. Not speaking up is unforgivable. Whether you are vegan, celiac, on a diet or you just can't eat something, you should let your host or hostess know beforehand if possible. The following these rules will help you get along anywhere. Practice them even when eating alone at home and soon they will become natural habits. Observe others.

Remain standing until all who are going to be seated are present. It there is a female on either side of you, assist them in seating by pulling the chair away from the table and then help them back to a comfortable space to eat. Then seat yourself and when seated, sit straight, do not slump in your seat.

Never start eating until all are seated. The host or hostess should take the first bite.

Eat whatever is served on your plate. If your dinner is already on the plate and served, eat whatever is served, whether you like it or not. You do not have to eat it, all but try to say nothing. It is okay to leave some on your plate.

Always pass to your left or clockwise. Not passing the right way? All food and condiments should be passed around the table clockwise. When you are passed an item that you do not care for, simply continue moving it around the table. If you are passed a pitcher or gravy dish, always turn it so the next person can receive it handle first. If you are the middle person delivering a plate on the request of the person sitting next to you, it's considered bad manners for you to do a little rest stop and take some for yourself. Salt and pepper always travel together regardless of which one was asked for. You should try everything; you may like it. As you mature, your tastes will change. Try everything.

Chew with your mouth closed and do so quietly. Do not smack. Don't talk with your mouth full. No one wants to see what you're eating.

Soup is to be taken with the large soup spoon. It is the large one on the right of your plate or bowl. Do not slurp soup or any beverage. Do not lean or hover over the bowl and spoon it up. Sit up and lean slightly forward is okay.

Wait until all are served before beginning each course.

Never speak with your mouth full. Wait until you have swallowed.

Never pick your teeth, sniff or blow your nose, scratch your ears or anything else at the table. Excuse yourself and leave the room.

Never discuss subjects that can be offensive at the table.

Never lick your fingers. Use a napkin.

Elbows do not belong on the table at any time.

Excuse yourself from the table when finished and then only when an emergency

exists. Otherwise, remain at the table until all are finished eating.

Offer to help with the dishes. Unless it is a formal dinner.

Rule of Thumb: EAT WHATEVER IS SERVED WHETHER YOU LIKE IT OR NOT. YOU MIGHT LIKE IT!

Chapter Six — Shoe Box Management

There are always those things that one wants to keep, regardless of what they may be. They cost money, why waste it? Perhaps, it's a memory, or a theatre program. Extra shoe strings, pins or buttons, maybe some aspirin you needed at one time. You may want it or may need it. I have lots of things that are like that. There is a way to keep and store them and find them when you want them. The secret is: *organize them*.

Many stores have a lot of plastic containers that are great for this type of storage. The following are examples of things and how to organize them. I like the large pencil box containers for storage which can be stacked inside of a larger plastic tub, and then stored nicely under your bed or in a closet. The small boxes are clear, so you can see what it in them, but label them nonetheless. The idea is that you don't go out and buy them, but as you need them. Shoe boxes will work initially.

The only exception to this is you need to buy a travel kit or Dopp kit for toiletries. As mentioned previously, this you will use the rest of your lives. Initially, buy a cheap one. This is for your day-to-day usage and will get you in the habit of knowing what you have and where it is. As you start to mature, it will become increasingly more important to you for shaving—sorry, you can't put it off. You will shave. The nice part is you can grab and go when necessary and you will have what you need. This is essential.

Other things you don't need daily but will need at some point in time are the things we are addressing now. When you must take care of yourself, and be responsible, you will greatly appreciate what we are saying. When a button falls off your only shirt, it is comforting to know that you have a replacement. If you don't know how to sew—learn. It isn't that hard.

When you accidentally cut yourself, it's nice to know you have a Band Aid. When you are invited to go someplace that is a little dressy, that you have a nice set of clothes and a way to clean your shoes. These are things that make you responsible and respectable.

This is "shoe box storage" and is not necessarily a shoe box but may be clear plastic containers with stackable lids. It is a means to organize what you have and/or need. It is a compact and efficient way to store them. They can be slide under your bed or in your closet and not take a lot of room.

There are ten of them and are as follows:

Shoe Box NO. 1: "SHOES." What else, but shoe polish and cleaners? Shoe polish is expensive, and you should have one for the color of your shoes. If you have black shoes, then black. If you have a pair of brown, then brown, and so forth. There are three basic colors: black, brown and cordovan (Oxblood), which are popular. You don't need all of these at once, but as you acquire things, this is the place you store what you need. I prefer *Kiwi Polish* which has been around for years. It keeps for years. It is available most any place that sells shoe maintenance items. When you buy a pair of shoes, it is wise to buy a matching shoe polish at that time.

You need a piece of terry cloth (old hand towel or washcloth) to apply it. You need a brush to brush them then and soft cloth to buff them shiny and clean. You may need white polish or a variety of other colors, depending on your shoes. Here's what the inventory of the contents looks like:

    1 – Black shoe polish

    1 – Brown shoe polish

    1 – Oxblood shoe polish

    1 – Shoe brush

    1 – Terry cloth towel

    1 – Polish applicator for each color

    1 – Suede brush [a small brass bristled brush]

Extra shoe strings. These will easily fit into a box.

Shoe Box NO. 2: "CLOTHES." The "clothes" box contains items that are used for maintaining your clothing: a sewing kit, which consists of small spools of thread and a needle with a few buttons, thread, a pin cushion with needles and pins, safety pins, spare buttons—never throw away an article of clothing without cutting the buttons off them first. You may or may not need them. It's always nice to have them when you do need them. A clothes or lint brush, a pair of scissors, a cloth tape measure. These are things that one needs all the time, but you really don't think about it — until you do.

Shoe Box NO. 3: 'MEDICINE,' prescription and non-prescription, vitamins, antacids, aspirin or headache remedies, antibiotic ointments, medicated powders, etc.

Shoe Box NO. 4: "FIRST AID," including bandages, *Band Aids*, gauze, *Vaseline*, antibiotic medication. Emergency type stuff. Even things that are used for wrapping a sprain that are reusable.

Shoe Box NO. 5: "BATHROOM" Which includes over stock stuff, like soap when you buy a three-pack and are using one, shampoo, toothpaste, spare toothbrushes, disposable razors, Chapstick, etc.

Shoe Box NO. 6: "SCHOOL SUPPLIES," like pencils, pens, erasers, paper clips, rulers, staples, *Scotch* tape, Post-it's, paper, envelopes, postage stamps, note pads, clips, rubber bands, blank labels, etc. As you grow older, these may change to Office Supplies.

Shoe Box NO. 7: "MISCELLANEOUS," Just Stuff. Scrapbook stuff, old tickets, photos, bobbles and pins, souvenirs, etc.

Shoe Box NO 8: "COMPUTER STUFF," including cords/cables, connectors, cell phone chargers, adapters, etc.

Shoe Box NO. 9: "TOOLS." Another group of things will be tools. These eventually belong in a toolbox, whether a plastic one or a metal one. You will start to acquire tools. Keep them all together. It may be a screwdriver or a hammer, pliers, etc. A good source for these can be found at garage or estate sales for much less.

Shoe Box NO. 10: "GAMES AND TOYS." Another aspect of life are games, cards, and toys. Keep these in another container or tub, like a "toy box," which will soon be a thing of the past. You may want to keep them, and you may not, you may want it for a memory. That's okay. You may have a lot of video or media drives, tapes or CD's. Do you want them? Just mark the tub: GAMES AND VIDEO. I have several games that I keep out like a nice chess set, special checkers, ivory dominos, and a deck of cards.

As you get older and go from high school to college or out on your own, these boxes and a tool box should remain constant. These are your things — they are not your parents. You will have what you need, when you need it. You will find that these items will go with you throughout your life. The contents may vary, the containers will get bigger, even into drawers, but the overall categories will remain the same.

People will respect you for your organization and wisdom. You will even be impressed when an emergency arises, and you have what you need.

Paperwork and Files. Just as you have your shoe boxes, you will learn that you also need to start saving a few more things like "papers." You will undoubtedly need insurance, automobile information and warranties, medical information, birth certificate, social security card, school records and diploma, titles and deeds, income and financial records, tax information, payment records and receipts, and the list goes on.

Some of it you can store on your cell or mobile phone, but most of it you must keep in hard copy format. Start early, and form the habit of organizing it. Create files for these materials. There are also "file boxes" which are available and portable and you can find these at garage or estate sales for near to nothing. These too, will go with you for the rest of your life. You won't need much at first, but you'll be amazed at how rapidly you start to acquire papers and documents.

These are things that we have always depended on our parents to do, or find, and take care of. As you grow and begin to be responsible, you must take over this aspect of your own life.

There are three books which you should have as well. These are: 1) a Bible, 2) Dictionary, and 3) Thesaurus. They will serve you well throughout your life.

> *Rule of Thumb: To find it when you need it, know where you put it.*

Chapter Seven — Substance Abuse

TEMPTATION. Young people have temptation coming at them from every angle. Adult beverages such as beer, wine, vodka, whiskey, rum, scotch, gin, anything with alcohol in it are ever present — *Try me.* Cigarettes and tobacco products are also there — *Try me.* Vaping E-cigarettes, a recent addictive action, is increasingly becoming more dangerous — *Try me.* Drugs are everywhere these days — *Try me.* Your hormones are raging, and the temptation is there for sex – *Try me.* There is a cost and it may be much more than you bargained for. It could destroy your life. In the case of sex, it could destroy two people's lives and change the course of your careers and history.

Don't "Try Me," Don't Start!

Vaping has grown in popularity with the rise of e-cigarettes. According to Linda Richter, PhD, Director of Policy Research and Analysis at the Center on Addiction, a growing body of evidence indicates that vaping products may be dangerous. Some people use these devices to vape THC, the chemical responsible for most of marijuana's mind-altering effects. Despite early optimism when these products first came on the market in the late 2000s, health advocates now recommend caution in using them in light of growing evidence suggesting that the risks, especially to young people, outweigh the benefits.

Vaping may cause nausea, vomiting, abdominal pain, and eye irritation. High doses of nicotine may cause tachycardia, high blood pressure, seizures, coma, and death.

The newest and most popular vaping product is JUUL, which is a small, sleek device that resembles a computer USB flash drive. Its subtle design makes it easy to hide, which helps explain why it has become so popular among middle and high school students. Every JUUL product contains a high dose of nicotine, with one pod or flavor cartridge containing about the same amount of nicotine as a whole pack of cigarettes.

The easiest to get are cigarettes. Heets are classified as cigarettes and produced by Phillip Morris. They are also highly addictive. Nicotine is easy to get addicted to and very difficult to give up. I see young people more and more smoking cigarettes. Being a former smoker myself, I know the perils that lie ahead. It was "cool" to smoke.

Cigarettes were being pushed at everyone in the movies—every scene. When you look at older movies, almost every scene had people either smoking a cigarette or having a "cocktail." It was considered sophisticated. Well, it wasn't and still isn't.

The price of cigarettes has gone from 18 cents a pack to nearly $8.00 per pack, and in some areas over $20.00 per pack, in my lifetime.

The person who smokes just one cigarette a day, finds that in another day or week or month they are smoking two and then it goes until they're smoking a pack a day. The average smoker goes through at least a pack a day. That's $240 per month. Some smokers go through two or three packs a day. That's $480 to $1800 per month. That's a lot of money going up in smoke. It would have bought some very nice things. By the end of the first year, that's $2,880.00 to $8,640.00, and where they are $20 per pack, up to $21,600 annually. It could have been payments on a nice car.

All smokers clothes stink, their hair stinks, their breath stinks, their hands and teeth are stained, their skin begins to get tiny wrinkles, they hack up brown congestion, and they're headed for lung or throat cancer. Very sophisticated! Who could get close to, or romantic with, someone like this, or even consider kissing them?

Same with liquor. It's very expensive, and you're destroying your youth. Drugs are destroying your life.

What do you do if you are hooked? Get help. There are professional organizations and medical facilities that specialize in addictions. The Department of Health and Human Services (HHS) has the Substance Abuse and Mental Health Services Administration. Helpline: 1-800-662-HELP (4357). They will help you find treatment.

Rule of Thumb: Control things that could and will control you.

Chapter Eight — Money Management

For most young men, money doesn't come easily. Jobs are difficult to find and the cost of living, dating, recreation and maintenance keeps us from saving a lot. One of the first things you need to do when you get a job, is to open a bank account, preferably a Savings Account. This will take a minimum amount of money, say $100. Add to this each month, and don't take it out of the bank, except in a bona fide emergency. *Not just that you're out of money*.

If you also open a checking account, there is a charge for this account. However, the convenience of having the ability to write checks is sometimes worth the minimum charge. Check what is available at your local bank.

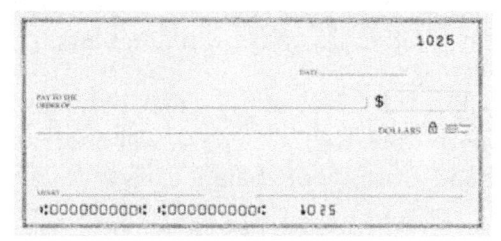

Writing a Check. The convenience of writing a check is that you are using the bank to pay your bills, so you don't have to carry money with you. By writing a check, you are authorizing the bank to pay the bill in the amount that you authorize from your account. For doing that, they will make a charge to you. When you open an account, they will give you checks which have a series of numbers across the bottom of the check which identifies the bank and its routing number; your account and the number of the check.

You write the date in the upper right hand by month, day and year. The next line down, starting at the left side, you identify who or what you are having the bank pay, then the numeric dollar amount. The next line down is for you to write out the amount such as: One Hundred and 00/100 Dollars. The next lines are MEMO: for you to identify what it is for, and then sign the check with your official signature which is on file with the bank.

When the recipient of the check deposits the check in the bank, your bank will deduct the amount from your balance, add a small charge for handling the check, and will send you a statement at the end of the month.

Credit Cards. These are the easiest, most convenient and most dangerous form of making payment. When starting out, you will be given a "credit limit." Let us say $500, which is the amount they are willing to loan to you. Let us also say that you need a pair of shoes, $75. You hand the sales clerk your credit card, and the bank verifies that there are "sufficient funds" in the bank to authorize it. It will be deducted from the $500 limit. You take your new shoes and leave. You want to take your friend to the movies and the ticket price is $15. You hand the ticket person your credit card, and they make a charge of $30 for the two tickets. That bank reduces the costs from the limit amount. You now have $105 less in your credit limit. At the end of the month, the bank will show you what your balance is and you have two choices: pay off the amount on the credit card and there is probably no service charge, or you can make minimum payment and carry the amount over. For that, there is a service charge.

The bank is glad to let you carry it over until the next month or for the next year. Soon you're in debt to the bank for the same amount as the limit, $500, plus all the interest and service charges. They might even increase your credit limit, and you may owe more than you make; this is the dangerous part.

The secret is that you pay off your credit charges every month. The banks don't like it, but you owe them nothing and you are debt free.

Debit Cards. Debit cards are like a check and allow you to pay your bills from your account. Unlike a credit card which pays the vendor from a loan amount, the debit cards withdraw from your own money.

ATM. Is an Automated Teller Machine. They are located in many places throughout an area. An ATM is an electronic banking outlet that allows customers to complete basic transactions without the aid of a branch representative or teller. Anyone with a credit card or debit card can access most ATMs.

Cost of Living. Whether you live at home or on your own. It's going to take money to live. There are costs for the house payments, including interest on the loan if the house is not paid for, taxes, insurance for fire, flood, liability for accidental injury, and other related items. Then there are utilities such as electricity for lights, cooking, microwave, air conditioning; water for drinking, cooking, bathing, washing; gas for heating, cooking, and ventilation. There are also costs for laundry soap, and clothes softeners, bleach, bathing soap, dishwashing, paper products like paper towels, toilet tissue, and Kleenex. Then there are the costs for food, spices, cooking oil, and the list goes on. Oh, yes, then there is furniture, beds, linens, towels, stoves, refrigerators, freezers, and still the list goes on. These are the things that as children, we take for granted.

As a youth growing up, many must share a small portion of what they make to stay at home. It's called "Room and Board." They don't make much money; however, there is a cost for you at your parents' house, so it is fair that you help.

Some are lucky, and their parents provide these to them for free while they are getting on their feet or going through school. If you live with your parents, there is also a responsibility: you must live by your parents' rules. It's a trade-off.

Additionally, there may be car payments and insurance premiums — and upkeep, gasoline and maintenance and tires. There are student costs for computers and related items, books and supplies, student loan payments, health care costs and insurance premiums, taxes and unforeseen events we often called, "rainy days."

WELCOME TO THE REAL WORLD!

It's not all fun and games. One realizes this when they get their first pay check. It's not all there, because around 20% of it is taken out for taxes and other mandatory requirements.

Then there are those necessities we tend to overlook—the nickel-and-dime items that add up to the dollars that seem to disappear. Like a coke and hot dog, a candy bar or a bag of potato chips. The package of gum or bag of popcorn. Or for dry cleaning a shirt or sports coat, that cost several dollars each. Sometimes it is a tube of toothpaste that costs two or three dollars or deodorant that costs three to five dollars.

Budgeting is something that you must do, whether you like it or not. You can only spend so much, or you'll find you're out of money before you thought you'd be.

You need to learn to "cut corners." Start with clothing—stick with wash and wear. Dry cleaning costs a lot, even the discounted places. You can do a lot of laundry for a fraction of the cost of dry cleaning. Some dry cleaning you must do like sports coat or good dress slacks. Keep these to a minimum. It may be the difference between eating or wearing something dirty.

Shoes should be of good quality and well maintained. Buy a classic style and keep them up, and they will last for years. Fad or the "latest style" shoes are usually here today and gone tomorrow and generally wear out before their time. Maybe you aren't really in style, but you won't ever be out of style either.

Don't blow a week's salary on anything; divide it wisely. A realistic formula if you're living at home would be as follows:

- · 50% on Cost of Living;

- 25% on Recreation;

- 15% on Clothes;

- 10% on Savings. Get in the habit of saving. If you can have it taken out of your pay check to start, you'll never miss it. Otherwise take it from the top.

As you can see, there isn't a lot left. A good rule of thumb when you're considering purchasing something: Do I need it, or do I want it? If you've lived this long without it, you probably don't need it. How badly do you want it? Is it worth doing without something else? Save your money and think about it. Don't be impulsive.

Community Living: You are now growing up. You've become young adults and with that comes responsibility. Prepare yourself for it and accept it gladly. You'll have a far better life if you do.

Some of you will go on to college, some military service. Others will consider marriage and entering the work world.

Whatever you do:

- Choose the people you wish to be like and live accordingly;

- Protect your record, *it will follow you the rest of your life — you will never escape it;*

- Establish your beliefs and standards;

- Define your morals and ethics — then live up to them;

- Don't let anything or anyone bring you down;

- Think of the other person and their feelings;

- Giving is better than getting;

- Do unto others as you would have them do unto you.

Things my mother taught me

While growing up, there were two sayings pasted on my bedroom mirror: *"The world owes no one a living; it was here first,"* and *"You are judged by the company you keep."*

Nothing is free, you get what you work for and don't hang around with people that can cause you trouble. Both have proven to be true. Another one that I learned from living: *"One can be a bystander for only so long."* Stay away from temptation. Otherwise it will catch you when you least expect it.

> ***Rule of Thumb: The world owes no one a living; it was here first.***

Chapter Nine — Learning to Communicate

When my son was about sixteen, he came to me and asked if we could talk. Naturally, I said of course. Then he burst into tears and hugged me and my heart broke. He said that he didn't fit in anywhere, he wasn't like other kids.

My son was in a talented and gifted school, and his classes were quite advanced. The long and short of it was that he was a "geek." He had nothing to talk about except his schooling. It's difficult to speak in Latin to a bunch of regular guys. He, like myself, was not an athletic person. He was strictly academic and knew of no other way. I asked him how many others in his class that were the same way. He replied, *"Most of them!"*

The next few days we spoke of a variety of things, and I came up with something that we called *"Life Preparation."* These weren't complex, but something that the Talented and Gifted program, through their advanced curriculum do not address. In my day, they called these Liberal Arts, which covered several things including music, theatre, art appreciation. We took that concept and added sports and a few more subjects.

The concept was that you do not have to play sports, but learn what the major leagues consist of, who they are, and where they stand for the season. Learn the rules. For example:

NFL (National Football League)

AFC (American Football Conference)
16 Teams
NFC (National Football Conference)
16 Teams
Total Teams in the NFL:
32 Teams

AFC East	**What City or State?**
Patriots	New England - Boston
Dolphins	Miami
Bills	Buffalo
Jets	New York

AFC North
Steelers	Pittsburg
Ravens	Baltimore
Bengals	Cincinnati
Browns	Cleveland

Who Am I? What Am I? What Do I Want To Be...When I Grow Up?

AFC South
Texans   Houston
Titans   Tennessee - Nashville
Colts   Indianapolis
Jaguars   Carolina

AFC West
Chiefs   Kansas City
Chargers   Los Angeles
Broncos   Denver
Raiders   Oakland

NFC East
Cowboys   Dallas
Eagles   Philadelphia
Redskins   Washington, DC
Giants   New York

NFC North
Bears   Chicago
Vikings   Minnesota
Packers   Green Bay, WI
Lions   Detroit

NFC South
Saints   New Orleans
Panthers   South Carolina
Buccaneers   Tampa Bay
Falcons   Atlanta

NFC West
Rams   Los Angeles
Seahawks   Seattle
Cardinals   Phoenix
49ers   San Francisco

Don't be afraid to ask questions and find someone who knows about the various sports. Learn the rules and watch a few games with them. Learn where they stand currently for the season, etc. This gives you something to talk about, but not to everyone. You can do the same for the National Basketball Association, National Hockey League, Major League Baseball, Golf, etc. Identify the Game, some of the players, and the rules.

Just as you do for sports, let's take **Movies**. What are the top ten box office hit movies? What are they about, and who are the major stars?

The same applies for the following:

Television Programs, Series or Movies
    Top Ten
    Top Ten Actors or Directors

Music Recordings/Artists
    What are the various genres?
    Top Singers and Producers

Concerts, Theatre, Musicals and Plays
    Top Shows
    Top Performers or Actors

Books *If you don't know about libraries, do so. You may discover a whole new world.*
>Bestsellers (Read what they are about)
>Who are the authors?

NASCAR and Racing
>What's it about?
>Who are the drivers?

These will enable anyone to speak or converse with almost anyone at a party or any place else for that matter. There are more things you can do as well, do you swim, play tennis, play golf, ski, boating, and the list goes on. Do you garden or grow things? Look at what you do (other than study), and learn to talk about it.

Ask questions of others. Find out what they do and learn from them. What do they like?

Perhaps your dad can be of help. If not, maybe it's something you can do together. If your dad isn't around, find an older person who can mentor you, or learn with you.

> ***Rule of Thumb: Live and learn, or just live.***

A wonderful book on communication is: *Why Am I Afraid to Tell You Who I Am?* by John S. Powell.

Chapter Ten — Spirituality

Your faith is very personal and something few talk about, yet everyone has an opinion about it as well. It is up to you as to what you believe. It is your choice. As you should know by now, life is a series of choices, and you must live by the results of those choices. Faith is believing in something unseen. In this country, it is a protection afforded by the US Constitution. You can be whatever you choose and have the freedom to worship however you want. It is the belief in something bigger than yourself a supreme being. You have freedom of religion, not freedom from religion.

As for me, I believe in God, the father almighty, creator of heaven and earth. I believe in Jesus Christ his only son, our Lord, who was conceived by the power of the Holy Spirit and born of the Virgin Mary. He suffered under Pontius Pilate, was crucified, died and was buried. He descended to the dead. After three days, he arose and ascended to Heaven and sits at the right hand of the Father. He will come again to judge the living and the dad. I believe in the Holy Spirit, the holy catholic church, the communion of saints, the forgiveness of sins, the resurrection of the body and the Life everlasting. Amen.

That makes me a Christian; a follower of the Lord Jesus Christ. I have been all my life and will continue to until the last breath. With this comes a guide book, *The Holy Bible*. It is filled with wonderful stories; the entire history of the world from its creation. It's a book that gives me a set of rights and wrongs called the Ten Commandments:

- I am the Lord, your God. You shall not worship false gods but adore Me alone and love Me above all things;

- You shall not take the name of the Lord, you God, without respect;

- Remember that you keep holy the Lord's Day;

- Honor your father and mother;

- You shall not kill;

- You shall not commit adultery;

- You shall not steal;

- You shall not bear false witness against your neighbor;
- You shall not covet your neighbor's wife;
- You shall not unjustly desire what belongs to your neighbor. Exodus 20:1-17.

These are the first guidelines that I must follow and are the basis for the laws in the United States. The second set of commands were by Jesus Christ who told us to "Love your God with all your strength, heart and mind, and love your neighbor as yourself."

Jesus took on the sins of the world and was crucified. Those sins died on the cross at Calvary, not in part, but the whole. If I believe in Jesus Christ, I will go to heaven, which is a far better place than this earth. I believe in one baptism and the power of prayer, it is the way I communicate with God the Father, Jesus the Son and the Holy Spirit, the three-in-one.

Jesus taught us how to live a perfect life and was loyal to his Father, even unto his death on the cross. He had twelve apostles, who were ordinary men. One betrayed him and hung himself. One of the greatest apostles was Paul, who had been Saul and persecuted Christ. He converted, changed his name and became the greatest of all; writing a good portion of the Bible's New Testament.

There are a lot of things one must do and not do. God has given us free will, and it is up to us to decide whether we will follow his commandments, teachings and wisdom. I choose to try. I believe that the Bible is the word of God. There are many versions; however, they all say essentially the same thing.

No human can live up to the perfection of Christ; therefore, we are all sinners. Belief in Christ and that he died for our sins, saves us all.

As for me and my house, we will serve the Lord. Joshua 24:15

Rule of Thumb: What you do is your choice.

Chapter Eleven — Sexuality

Everyone has needs, and Abraham Maslow, a psychologist who is best known for his *Hierarchy of Needs* published in 1954. His works have proven over and over to be right on. I am simplifying if for the purpose of writing this chapter.

Level 1: These are the physiological or base needs for survival. One cannot exist without them: Air for breathing, food, water, clothing, shelter, sleep and sex. These must be obtained to live. Without these needs being met, one cannot think beyond them.

Sex — a basic and survival need of mankind. You are either taught about it in a controlled environment or learn it from the streets. It is uncomfortable for most to talk about, especially to your own parents, and them to their kids. People don't for that reason. The kids are on their own. When I was growing up, sex was never mentioned, in fact it was almost forbidden. It wasn't something you talked about. The perception is — it's dirty. It really isn't, but we treat it that way.

Why is that very thing that expresses love, produces children and is a basic need of mankind not talked about? I guess it is the awareness of the passage of time for our children. It is difficult for a parent to let go of their child's childhood and see them cross over into adulthood.

As a boy reaches the age of eleven or twelve he begins to develop hormones which take control of seemingly everything. He starts growing hair from under his arms, he grows it in his pubic area, on his legs, arms and face. Some boys more than others. The time frame varies as well. I jokingly call it the *"Charming Age of Puberty."* For it is the opposite from being charming. We become awkward, our voice begins to change to the lower register and we often develop skin conditions — acne.

Another area that begins to change is your penis. It changes in size as you mature. It also has some very new and strange feelings. You are sometimes told to not touch or feel himself or will face eternal damnation or some such story.

It is perfectly normal to touch or feel yourself. Masturbation is regarded as a normal, healthy sexual activity that is pleasant, fulfilling, acceptable, and safe. It is a good way to experience sexual pleasure and can be done alone throughout your life — and you don't even have to worry about bad breath or body odor.

It is only considered a problem when is done in public, it inhibits sexual activity with a partner, or causes significant distress to the person.

Dating: Just as a boy/young man begins to feel differently, so do the girls, and you put the two together, and here we go! Dating is as natural as homemade apple pie. There are a lot of places to be together to share a movie, the television, a snack bar, soda fountain, roller or ice skating, to be with friends, going to church and church activities. There are a lot of school activities as well. These are fun days filled with new adventures. Enjoy them, but also be aware that they can get you in trouble. Temptation is just around the corner. Don't let it catch you by surprise. You've got your whole life ahead of you. Don't make mistakes at this early juncture of life. Keep private things — private.

Holding hands, necking—kissing, these are normal and pleasant. Just avoid getting involved any more than this. For both of your sakes, learn to back off from situations that could lead further. When a girl says, "No," back off!

Recently, I heard about a sixteen-year-old girl from New England, living in a small town. She became pregnant and her family disowned her completely. They kicked her out of the house and made her go some other place to have the child. They never welcomed her back, leaving her to her own resources to raise the baby. She put the baby up for adoption. She turned to drugs and eventually killed herself. Sad story which could have been avoided. I don't know which is worse, her family that were mired in selfishness or the girl for allowing herself to get carried away in the passion of the moment.

Treat your body as a temple. Protect yourself and save yourself from situations that could steal it from you. Once your innocence is gone, what do you have to offer your true love when that happens?

We hear a lot about people who are: lesbian, gay, bisexual or transgender (LGBT). God is perfect, He doesn't make mistakes, so let's not be too hasty to draw conclusions about who is right and who is wrong — who is good and who is bad. The same rules in life apply to gays, lesbians, and transgender. Be loyal to your life partner. Be monogamous.

Do not be promiscuous, for it is through promiscuity that HIV and AIDS were initially spread. It killed hundreds of thousands — still does. It is a terminal disease, and there are some people who have it who don't care who they pass it on to.

There are several other sexually transmitted diseases (STDs): chlamydia, gonorrhoea, syphilis, herpes, and others, which are easily transmitted and difficult if not impossible to cure. Check them out on the Internet to find the symptoms, side effects and other information. There are other complications like crab lice, which can cause problems as well. Don't take chances, the odds are too great. If you find yourself in a situation and go the whole way, use a condom. They are available in any drugstore or pharmacy.

What do you do when it's too late — when you already have an STD? As embarrassing as it is, it was your choice — you made the decision. You've got to "face the music," tell your parents, and immediately seek medical assistance. All doctors and institutions are required to report the STDs to the Centers for Disease Control (CDC). They in turn will contact you and you must report all recent sexual activity giving the names of all participants who in turn will be contacted in order to stop the spread of the disease. It only gets more embarrassing.

What if your girlfriend is pregnant? Once again it was your choice and decision — and it's too late. Tell your parents, as there is no hiding it. Now there are major decisions to be made that will affect your entire life. You no longer have youth. You must become an adult and take on the whole responsibility. You have forever changed the life of the two of you. You have also limited whatever career opportunities you may have had.

Rule of Thumb: Save yourself, you'll be glad you did.

Chapter Twelve — Who Am I? What Am I? What Do I Want to Be When I Grow Up?

WHO AM I?

This is something that I struggled with for many years beyond my youth. It seems to start with self-esteem. Most younger teenagers are self-conscious, insecure and searching. They don't know who they are or where they fit in. There are always exceptions, but I believe this generally applies to most. This is a pattern that can continue for years after the teen years as well.

Part of this book is to help guide you through some of the processes to identify who you are. First, let us look at the Boy Scouts of America manual for the Scout Law, which defines basic or core descriptors:

> **TRUSTWORTHY.** Tell the truth and keep promises. People can depend on you. Show that you care about your family,

friends, Scout leaders, school, and country.

LOYAL. Show that you care about your family, friends, Scout leaders, school and country.

HELPFUL. Volunteer to help others without expecting a reward.

FRIENDLY. Be a friend to everyone, even people who are very different from you.

COURTEOUS. Be polite to everyone and always use good manners.

KIND. Treat others as you want to be treated. Never harm or kill any living thing without good reason.

OBEDIENT. Follow the rules of your family, school, and pack. Obey the laws of your community and country.

CHEERFUL. Look for the bright side of life. Cheerfully do tasks that come your way. Try to help others be happy.

THRIFTY. Work to pay your own way. Try not to be wasteful. Use time, food, supplies, and natural resources wisely.

BRAVE. Face difficult situations even when you feel afraid. Do what you think is right despite what others might be doing or saying.

CLEAN. Keep your body and mind fit. Help keep your home and community clean.

REVERENT. Be reverent toward God. Be faithful in your religious duties. Respect the beliefs of others.

These are the best examples of what you should be, or at least try to be. I can think of none better. If you are not a Boy Scout, maybe it's a good place for you to discover who you are. Is there a Boy Scout troop near you? Check it out. These eleven descriptors are the finest I know and will establish your core beliefs. They will help to define your character.

Second, let us look at what your strengths and weaknesses are. These will require you to sit and think for a while. Don't even try this until you have at least two hours to dedicate to the task. Go to a quiet place with no distractions and take a pad of paper and a pencil or pen.

Start with your strengths. Just use one to three-word descriptors: Tall, nice looking, red-headed, good complexion, smart, intelligent, good singer, and so forth. Be honest with yourself.

Then do the same for your weaknesses. Such descriptors would be: talk too much, easily distracted, don't pay attention, etc.

In a couple of hours, you should have a good list of both. What we are going to do is to focus on the Strengths and make them stronger. The Weaknesses are something that we need to be aware of, but unless they take away from your Strengths, work on those when you have nothing else to do or they really bother you.

An example of this would be that Thomas Alva Edison, knew absolutely nothing about the tribal habits of the Walla Walla tribe of Native Americans in Spokane, Washington. Should he have taken his time to learn what they were, or focus on that which he did best — invent things?

The idea is contrary to our society today, which focuses on the negative aspects of life. "Don't do this," and "Don't do that." Or, "You shouldn't do...whatever." These are negative, and we don't want to hear them.

We're going to take the positive approach and focus on strengthening our strength. This list is what's good about us, and what we do well. Let's use this list to see where we want to take it.

These are the things that will help us gain confidence and raise our self-esteem. Feel good about yourself. Like yourself, for if you don't, who can? Like who you are and what you believe. Be proud of yourself. Do the best you can with what you've got.

Identify those qualities and characteristics that you most want to be like. Which ones do you want to have define you? When people get to know you, how would you like them to describe you?

This is the beginning of who you are. *You're okay, I'm okay.*

WHAT AM I?

Knowing who you are, will define what you are. What do you want to be? Set your mind to it and go for it. Whatever you do best, make it better—be the best. If you can sing, find out where you can take singing lessons to become better. If you are good at playing baseball, talk to your coach, and find out where you can become better. Pick someone you admire, and figure out what you admire about them. Then be like them. The greatest form of flattery is to have someone copy you.

Take your list and then add what you can do with each strength, and where it could take you. Use your imagination, and dream a little. You can be anyone or anything you choose to be.

WHAT DO I WANT TO BE WHEN I GROW UP?

This is one of my favorite things to do: set goals. It is not easy, but you need to start someplace. We are going to take your life and divide it into nine different categories and then determine what you want in each of those categories. Like making the list of strengths and weaknesses; don't cut your time short. It takes hours for this exercise.

1. **Status and Respect.** What do you expect from people and what do you want them to think about you? This

includes social status, status in your community, we are talking about lifetime achievement. Once you have done this, we are going to break this into segments of time:

a. **Micro.** What can you do about it today, this week or over the next month or so?

b. **Short Term.** What can you do over the next year to accomplish a portion of this goal?

c. **Mid-Range.** What can you do over the next one to three years?

d. **Long Range.** What can you do over the next five to ten years?

e. **Macro Goal.** What do you expect to be or accomplish as a lifetime goal?

By doing it in this manner, you can identify where you want to be at the end of your life and what you can do right now to achieve your goal.

2. **Personal Relationships.** What type of relationships do you expect from

friends, lovers, a wife, parents, family, acquaintances, co-workers, bosses, teachers, police, etc., during your lifetime? What can you do about it right now — **Micro**. Then **Short Term**, etc.

3. **Leisure Satisfactions and Recreation/Hobbies.** What do you enjoy doing now that you'd like to do the rest of your life? Swimming, boating, baseball, collecting things, gardening, golfing, tennis, whatever. When you reach the later years, what would you like to be doing? Now, what can you do in the **Micro**, **Short Term**, etc., to achieve this goal?

4. **Education and Learning.** Let say you want to be a teacher. What's it going to take for you to become one? It's going to take a degree or perhaps several. What is the time-frame? What can you do today — **Micro**, **Short Term**, etc. What if you want to be a plumber, lawyer, doctor, or candlestick maker? What's it going to take to achieve that goal and what can you do today?

5. **Spiritual Growth (Spirituality).** What are your beliefs, religion, faith and acceptance of a higher power or none? Where do you see yourself over the course of your life and how would you like it to be in the **Micro, Short Term**, etc.

6. **Work Satisfaction — Career.** What are your career goals? What do you think you want to be? Doctor, lawyer, merchant, thief? Butcher, baker and candlestick maker, what are your lifetime goals? What can you do about it today — **Micro, Short Term**, etc.

7. **Material Wealth and Possessions.** Dream, what do you want to have? A beautiful house on a lake, a fancy car, furniture, money in the bank? Do you want to be the richest person in the world? How are you going to do that? What can you do today — **Micro, Short Term**. Etc.

8. **Health and Physical Fitness.** These are all the things you need to do to have good health and to be physically fit throughout your lifetime. If you

want to be able to climb Mt. Everest at fifty, you need to stay physically fit and healthy. What are the things you need to do over the time periods, **Micro, Short Term, Mid-Range**, etc.

9. **Political Identity.** Do you want to be Conservative or Liberal and do you want to get into politics? Find out what a Conservative is and what a Liberal is. How do you get involved over the **Micro, Short Term**, etc.

As you can see, this is a very detailed project and one that takes a lot of thought. It will take you many weeks if you do it right. Then you must look and see if there are conflicts, e.g., to save $5,000 and buy a new car at the same time. You can't do both. There may be supportive goals as well, like learning to play golf and meeting someone important — who likes to play golf? Ah, Ha!

You plan your work and work your plan. You plan your life and then live it. Make it happen. It does work, I know — because I did it.

If you need help, find a mentor who will work with you. If you need advice, seek counsel.

Don't be afraid to ask questions. The dumbest question is the one you don't ask.

Rule of Thumb: To make it happen, plan it! For if you don't write it down and plan it, it is only a dream.

Chapter Thirteen — Preparing to Live on Your Own

As you grow, mature and leave home, there are a lot of things you are going to have to learn how to do that you have depended upon your parents to do for you.

College: If you are going to college away from home, you are going to need certain basic items and will have limited storage space. In all probability you will be sharing your room with a roommate. You simply can't save everything, and you cannot afford to buy new things as you need them. As we discussed in the chapter five about Shoe Box Management, there is a way to have what you need and when you need it. You can easily take your plastic tub with the shoe boxes in it and slip it under your bed.

However, you will need to know how to sew on a button, or to hem a cuff on your pants. Do you know how? You won't have mom there to do it for you. You'll be glad you have a sewing kit and the necessary items to sew. Take the time to learn how to do them now. It isn't that hard. You won't be able to rely on your roommate or someone else.

Mom won't be there to clean your room or make your bed or do your laundry either. Take the time now to learn how to run the washing machine and dryer; how to iron clothes and put them away. Learn how to make a bed, and to take care of your clothes with a place for the dirty ones and learn how to fold and store the clean ones.

You're also going to have to learn how to clean a bathtub or shower as well as a sink and toilet. You will learn that *Febreze* is your best friend.

House or Group House: The same rules that apply above also apply in a House, Group House or apartment; however, there are additional responsibilities: Cooking and house cleaning and often making minor repairs. You won't have mom or dad there either. You must do it yourself.

Learn the basics of cooking, shopping to cook, food preparation, and what goes in the refrigerator. How to prepare meat and store it. What cooking utensils one needs and how to use them. How to boil, bake, broil, pan fry, simmering, steaming, microwaving, grilling, etc. What pans to have. Essential basic things like sugar, salt, pepper, flour, dairy products like milk, cream, eggs; condiments like mayonnaise, ketchup, mustard; bread and buns; sandwich meat; etc.

Learn what kind of fast foods you can fix on the run. You won't be able to rely on anyone but yourself, and you can't afford to buy all your meals out. You'll probably want water, soft drinks, and other standard stuff. Learn now — how to be independent.

What about minor repairs? You're going to have to make them yourself. You'll be glad you have a Toolbox. You're going to need basic tools and miscellaneous items such as: a hammer, screwdrivers—both flathead and Phillips, they come in sets. You will need a pair of pliers, both regular and a pair of needle nose pliers, a pair of dike snippers, some type of drill, whether a Yankee type or an electric. You're going to need duct tape, nails, screws, bolts, and nuts, which can be kept in small jars; wood glue, 3-n-1 oil, WD-40 as well.

You will need a First Aid kit with band-aids, etc., for emergency cuts, bruises, burns, and other minor accidents.

The <u>No. 1 Shoe Box</u> is for shoe stuff. Do you know how to clean and polish shoes? If not now, when are going to learn?

Military: Some of you will go into the military: Army, Navy, Air Force, Coast Guard. You will be going through Basic Training, where you will be taught to be totally self-sufficient. You *will* make your bed, you *will* clean the barracks, you *will* sew, you *will* polish shoes and brass, you *will* keep your area neat and clean. You *will* not have anyone but yourself to do it.

You *will* be told what to wear and bring when you report to duty and take nothing else. You *will* have everything provided and told how to use it. You *will* be told how to shower, what to wear, and you *will* eat when and how, and where you *will* eat it. You *will* either eat it or go hungry. There is no place to buy what you would like. You *will* belong to Uncle Sam and do as you are told. It will make no exception who you are or what you've done — mom and dad have no influence, no connections and *will not* be able to do anything for you. You *will* show respect to your superiors — SIR!

To me, going in the military is the wisest choice of all, particularly if you cannot afford to go to college or don't know what you want. It teaches one to be independent, well trained, learning respect, have a purpose, and providing service to others. You will develop a sense of pride and self-respect and have the latitude to be whatever you choose. It provides you with free medical and gives you the opportunity to further your education and will even pay for it.

Living On Your Own: As you graduate from High School or take a job away from home, or for whatever reason, you may be faced with providing for yourself. You have no one to rely upon except yourself. It's scary. You are facing the unknown and facing it alone. Some are currently living in circumstances which are less than desirable. These are the times where planning and looking ahead are very important.

While you can, start planning on what you are going to do, where you are going to do it, and how to get from here to there. Money is number one. Save it! Unless you have an absolute need, save it. It will give you an independence to make the right decisions. A new or nice car would be great, but do you need it? It may take all your savings. Worse yet, it may put you into debt which has to be repaid, and you have no means to pay it back. This ruins your credit rating and you may spend the rest of your life trying to improve a bad one.

Moving out on your own can be exciting, but it doesn't just happen. You must plan on it and by making a good plan; it can all happen. You can do or be anything you choose.

These are the days for planning ahead. You are young and have the time to do it right. Will you? It's your choice.

Rule of Thumb: You are what you choose.

Printed in Great Britain
by Amazon